Distracted Driving:

The Multi-Tasking Myth

Steven D. Gacovino, Esq.

Edward Lake, Esq.

Luke W Russell

DEDICATION

To those who have suffered at the hands
of distracted drivers, and to those
who realize technology must not master us.

CONTENTS

Preface

We all like to think we're in control of our mind. It's kind of hard to imagine that we would be like the people who demonstrate in experiment after experiment that our attention easily gets away from us.

Who would think, for instance, that you could be told to keep an eye on a group of basketball players gathered together passing a couple basketballs while a gorilla walks onto the middle of the screen and waves at you – and yet you don't even notice the gorilla.

Many experiments have shown how easily our attention is diverted, while we go on thinking we are alert to what's right in front of us. We easily fail to see "obvious" things...including things that might need to be noticed while we're driving a car.

We all wonder who's having all those reported accidents blamed on texting or talking on cellphones while driving. Are those stupid drivers? Or are they distracted at just the moment when full attention is required?

The fact is that almost everyone can talk on a phone while driving without having a wreck. It's also a fact that attention spread too thin at critical moments is behind many accidents. That's what this little book is about – the critical moments when our full attention is required to operate a vehicle without causing harm to others or ourselves. The issue lies in those very short moments – not in the undeniable fact that we rarely have an accident while talking on the phone.

Accidents are called accidents because they are unusual. Someone slips on a small puddle of water on a restaurant floor because the puddle is nearly invisible, or steps on a nail in the grass at the city park.

Auto accidents rarely occur, compared to how many times we venture onto the roads. When we talk about accidents, we are talking only about rare moments. But cellphone use is making them less rare, enough less rare that we should drop our defenses and listen to evidence that says we are introducing a dangerous variable into our driving. It's a little bit like pouring ourselves a small puddle of water to slip on every once in a while, or tossing a nail into the grass and thinking that we won't step on it, since the park lawn is so big.

Do As I Say

En route to a recent conference for attorneys in Myrtle Beach, I, Luke, was enjoying the mid-afternoon flight and the beautiful autumn day on the other side of my airplane window. I walked out the airport terminal after landing and hopped into a taxi waiting for a visitor like me. The 40-minute drive was a cruise along broadleaf trees still dressed in green, unlike the Hoosier landscape I had left behind.

I struck up a conversation with the driver and learned that his grandkids badly needed an iPhone. He felt it was his responsibility to buy them one.

We talked about how much people use their phones, and we ended up on the topic of using a phone while driving. He explained to me, "I tell my family, 'When I'm driving, I won't pick up. If you need me, it can wait, because I gotta drive.'"

As I was agreeing, a ringtone sounded. "Hang on a sec," he said. To my amazement, he pulled a cellphone out of his shirt pocket and entered into a brief exchange on what sounded like a work-related matter. Then he put the phone back in his pocket and we continued talking – about other things.

Distracted driving has become a red-hot topic. It has also become an old topic. Everywhere you go it calls out from billboards, newspapers, magazines, banners inside malls, radio and TV. It's even painted on city buses.

Distraction.gov, a federally owned website, says "distracted driving is any activity that could divert a person's attention away from the primary task of driving." It goes on to say that, "because text messaging requires visual, manual, and cognitive attention from the driver, it is by far the most alarming distraction."[i]

When I set out to put this report and the corresponding video together, I planned to dig into data on accidents and fatalities blamed on distracted driving. Distraction.gov says, "The best way to end distracted driving is to educate all Americans about the danger it poses."[ii]

The site goes on to lists facts and statistics that it says are "powerfully persuasive." Unfortunately, some of the statistics are quoted out of context and some are unconvincing, no matter how startling they may be.

Consider the simple fact that 75% of American teens still say it's normal to text while driving, even though 97% of teens say texting while driving is dangerous.[iii] Adults too know about the dangers of using a cellphone while driving, and yet vehicle crashes involving cellphones result in 1,600,000 crashes annually, accounting for approximately 28% of all traffic accidents. [iv] Texting while driving makes you 23 times more likely to crash.[v]

Everybody hears the same statistics about the dangers of using cellphones while driving, but they use the phones anyway, even on motorcycles! Drivers use cellphones even though they know accidents are costly. In 2011, the average property damage associated with crashes was $9,100.[vi] That's more than most people want to spend on an unplanned event.

States have used the same "powerfully persuasive" data to enact laws on the use of a cellphone while driving. But vehicle accidents and fatalities attributed to using a cellphone do not seem to be declining.

Many companies, especially major cellular networks, conduct extensive campaigns against texting while driving. We hear those campaigns continually. We're quoted scary statistics and told "it's not worth it." While it's easy to agree with the sentiment, it would be nice to see quality data on the impact the statistics are having on driving behavior. I know plenty of responsible adults who talk on their cellphones – and sometimes text – while driving.

AT&T has a wonderful campaign that lets people tell personal stories of how distracted driving has negatively impacted their lives. The stories are told in many heart-wrenching videos, but they have not influenced a widespread change in behavior.

AT&T even ends phone conversations with their customers by encouraging them not to text and drive.

I struck up the following conversation only moments ago with Liz, a young stranger sitting near my table at a Starbucks cafe.

"Can I share something with you and get your reaction?" I asked.

"Sure!" she said.

"I was on the phone with a consultant today and as our conversation was coming to a close, something sparked her to say, 'Everyone here in San Diego texts while driving. We've got to multi-task and I guess we've got to do it somehow.'"

"Well," Liz started, "I can't say much, as I'm guilty too. I've texted on my phone while driving."

"If you know it is dangerous, why do you still text and drive?" I probed.

"Well, you know, I hear those ads where people talk about how they were texting and driving and killed three people and it's really powerful stuff." She paused for a moment.

"But it doesn't change your behavior, does it?"

"No, it doesn't."

Legislation, education, and strong stories may eventually play a major role in reducing the cellphone problem, but they are not the entire answer. As long as people think they are good multi-taskers, using a phone while driving only makes sense. Each of us needs to recognize a faulty assumption: *We think our attention to important tasks is not significantly diminished during multi-tasking, and so we assume we can pay adequate attention to the road and everything involved in safe driving, while doing whatever else we want to do.*

The next couple of chapters are meant to shed light on the negative impact of handling multiple tasks while driving.

A Quick Word about Texting and Driving

I, Steven, have a brother who owns an auto body shop. He told me recently that amidst all the safety features being implemented in cars, his business has grown, and he attributes the influx of cars to people's ever-increasing need to text and drive.

Many interesting conversations have taken place while assembling this book. Regarding texting and driving, there were usually two types of people: (1) those who believed it was irresponsible, and (2) those that believed it was dangerous but did it nonetheless.

The former group are always shocked when they are told that 18% of adults admit to texting or emailing while driving.[vii] The latter group would even go on to say, "I tell my kids not to text and drive and they say, 'Dad, you do it!'"

To our surprise, a third category of people believe that texting and driving is safe. You might think, "We need to educate them." As we said before, that's what the government has said the solution is. However, even in news articles about the dangers of texting and driving, individuals still contend that it's not a big deal for some.

In one CBS News article about the dangers of texting, someone made the following paraphrased comment:

"Some can multi-task better than others. There are some people that can text while driving and it is a minor distraction, while others have a hard time simply walking down the street and chewing gum at the same time."[viii]

Texting requires you to look, touch, and think outside of the scope of driving, so much so that the average text demands approximately 4.6

seconds of your visual focus. In other words, at the speed of 55 MPH, that's like driving the length of a football field with your eyes off the road.[ix]

If you're like others, you may argue the fact that while texting and driving, some people are continually moving their eyes back and forth from the road and their phone, so they are not driving an entire football field "blind," as some argue.

While that may very well be true, in the coming chapters we are going to address our multi-tasking capabilities. We will explore some studies conducted which analyze the weaknesses that we are usually unaware of.

Recently our firm resolved a claim involving a teenager who sustained serious cervical and lumbar spine injuries in a motor vehicle accident. The driver of the other vehicle was allegedly texting while driving. As a result, the young victim will live with the injuries for life.

Another thing to consider is that as of June 1, 2013, motorists in New York who are found guilty of texting or emailing while driving can receive five points on their license and be subject to a $150 fine. This is a stiffer penalty than someone found guilty of speeding 20 MPH over the speed limit.

Texting while driving is risky, unfair to others, and can cost you a lot of money.

Myth: Talking on the Phone
While Driving Is the Same
as Talking to a Passenger

Harvard Medical School psychologist Todd Horowitz and his colleagues found that common hands-free phone conversations impaired visual attention. They did not find impairment when they asked drivers to listen to a novel over the phone or simply to repeat the caller's words.

Horowitz explained, "It's not listening. It's not moving your mouth and making sounds and making words. It's that intervening bit, where you have to actually think about what you're going to say and generate some new content for whoever you're talking to."[x]

In Horowitz's study, volunteers participated in a test of visual attention, tracking moving objects on a computer screen. The purpose of the study was to see to what extent an everyday conversation over a hands-free phone would affect performance on the tracking activity. Sure enough, performance while on the phone dropped in comparison to when there were no phone distractions.

Next the volunteers listened to an audio book over the phone's speaker while performing the tracking task. Performance was not affected by the distraction. Participants were also asked to repeat words that a caller said over the phone. Again, the distraction did not affect performance.

Finally, the participants were asked to answer riddles over the phone while trying to track the objects on the screen. This is where the researchers concluded that having to think about what you're going to say during a conversation is a strong distraction. The riddle caused significant mental interference that hurt performance on the tracking task.

The result might lead you to conclude that talking to a passenger in the vehicle you're driving is the same as talking to someone on the phone while you're driving. However, Horowitz went on to explain what he calls "situational awareness."

He speculated that when you're talking to someone next to you, that person has an awareness of the situation you confront as the driver. The other person is able to take cues from the surrounding environment and behave accordingly. For instance, if traffic becomes intense when you're merging onto a freeway, your passenger is likely to stop talking or to slow the conversation down temporarily.

A person on the other end of a phone will not know to modify the conversation according to your driving situation. You will therefore have to divert your attention momentarily either to ask the person to stop talking or to let the person continue talking in your ear while you're trying to manage your entry onto the hectic freeway.

The extra set of eyes that a passenger brings can be very helpful. Those eyes may notice a pedestrian you don't see. Even though a conversation with your passenger will consume some of your attention, the extra set of eyes could help sustain or increase your awareness, helping you to make better driving decisions. The person talking to you on the cellphone does not provide the same assistance.

And you usually don't have to work as hard to hear a passenger as you do to work through the audio variation and distortion that are common on cellphones.

The point is that talking to a passenger is not the same as driving while talking on the phone.

Many drivers have argued that talking into a headset or other technology is safer than holding and talking into the phone. This past Thanksgiving a family member and I, Luke, were talking about distracted driving. A friend named John came along and wanted to know what I had been saying. After I told him, he said he was going to stop calling his wife, Samantha, on his way home from work, and he hoped she would stop calling him during the drive.

A few weeks later at another gathering, Samantha told me John had stopped answering her calls on his way home from work. I gently shared a few details about distracted driving, as I had done with John, and Samantha was intrigued. As she was telling me I should put this information together for a video or book, a friend of hers joined our conversation.

"Do you talk on the phone while you're driving?" Samantha asked him.

The man shifted his weight from one foot to the other and explained that his car has a device that lets him use his phone without touching it.

My research into the topic had made me more willing than I normally would be to talk about such things at a holiday get-together. I said, "The cognitive functions required for a conversation are the same whether you're holding the phone or talking through your car."

"But it *is* different!" he said.

Having 30 years more driving experience than I, he was certain that his car phone brought a commendable level of safety to his phone habit.

Psychologist Brian Scholl asked participants in one experiment to track objects on a computer screen. One group tracked the objects while maintaining a conversation on a cell phone. A second group tracked the objects but did not talk on the phone. At some point in the experiment, an unexpected objected appeared on the screen. Of the participants that were *not* conversing on the phone, 30% missed the unexpected object, whereas a full 90% of those who *were* talking on the phone missed the unanticipated object.[xi]

The study showed that cell phone conversations can dramatically affect our ability to see and notice our surroundings, even if we are directly looking at them, particularly unexpected elements.

The issue is not about whether we are able to hold a successful conversation on the phone while driving. The issue is about the effects of conversation on available cognitive resources in unexpected scenarios. By allowing conversations to consume our attention, we put ourselves and others at risk by limiting our ability to react.

In their book, *The Invisible Gorilla*, psychologists Daniel Simons and Christopher Chabris say there's an underlying assumption plaguing our human population: "Our vivid visual experience masks a striking mental blindness – we assume that visually distinctive or unusual objects will draw our attention, but in reality they often go completely unnoticed." [xii]

Simons and Chabris go on to state that drivers "assume they will notice – that as long as they are looking in the right direction, unexpected objects and events will grab their attention." [xiii] In the next chapter we will see that it is normal to be looking directly at something without noticing it.

Companies have tried to solve the dangers of cellphone use while driving by developing hands-free technologies. Hands-free does have a few benefits, such as not having to touch the device to dial or answer. But no matter how experienced drivers are, cellphone use introduces risk to the drivers and others by consuming part of the cognitive resources required for the many tasks that are part of safety on the road.

The argument that one technology is "safer" does not address the fact that by using the device you are introducing risks to yourself and others around you. You are increasing the likelihood of a mishap.

To address the issue of distracted driving, we must choose to reorient our perspective on these distractions. Until the past several years, people seldom used a phone while driving. Now that the technology has made it possible to use a phone everywhere you drive, the temptation to make excuses to use it are truly powerful.

"Less risky" technology has become widely popular, whereas hardly anyone was driving with a phone until fairly recently. "Needing" a phone everywhere we went was not part of our routine. "Needing" to keep in constant communication wasn't either. "Needing" to answer incoming calls on nonexistent phones wasn't part of daily life.

Nowadays we're used to having a cellphone accessible at all times, and we become unsettled when we don't know where it is. It's a tool we can't seem to function without. The urge to pick it up when it beeps or rings is powerful and even irresistible. This urge motivates many people to look for "less risky" technology to soothe their concerns about safety.

Multi-Tasking and
Inattentional Blindness

People often boast an ability to multi-task. They mean they're able to do more than one thing pretty well at a time. Women are often said to have a superior ability to multi-task. Have you talked to one recently who was handling several duties at one time – while you were trying to get information out of her, or telling her about something of interest to you and thinking she was hearing you? Mothers are usually more willing than fathers to multi-task, but that does not make them more attentive.

Attention has its limits – strict limits – and our culture's technology saturation is at an all-time high, spreading our attention, our awareness, more thinly than ever across more inputs and outputs. Yet many people still believe they are good multi-taskers.

Doing more than one thing at a time is ordinary, but doing more than one thing very well at the same time is another matter when those things demand concentration. When the brain attempts to devote its limited resources of attention to attention-demanding tasks, something is going to give. Something is going to get insufficient attention, if not ignored altogether.

MIT neuroscientist Earl Miller puts it bluntly: "You're not paying attention to one or two things simultaneously..." He says you're actually "switching between them very rapidly."[xiv]

For example, you cannot give all your attention to your cellphone while also listening closely to the car radio. You're not paying as much attention as you think when one of those tasks requires or automatically draws your strict attention. At such a moment, you are permitting a significant degree of interference, and it just so happens that many, many bad things happen in moments just like those.

Some tasks can be done with a high degree of automation – that is, without much conscious thought. A highly experienced driver, for instance, can steer around bumps in the road while remaining aware of the speed limit, better than a new driver can.

Nevertheless, even automated activity consumes a certain amount of our attention. Things we do very well – with little conscious thought – can take a big bite out of mental capacity.

Some people are more willing than others to multi-task, but their attention will still be spread unevenly across attention-demanding stimuli and tasks.

We're all the same in that way. It's a human thing. Willingness to multi-task doesn't change our limitations. Our resources of attention are limited by nature. Folding familiar laundry may seem to be the easiest thing in the world, as easy as talking on the phone, as easy as driving may seem; yet all highly familiar tasks use a measure of mental capacity. They can devour our attention as easily as other tasks, depending on how our attention is directed or drawn.

A driver's attention is cast and drawn across multiple stimuli and tasks: road signs; GPS systems; beautiful scenery; drivers in the next lane; the slow driver we're going to pass as soon as we get a chance; thinking about our plans for the day; conversation with passengers; the signal on the cellphone that tells us we have a message or a call. All of these are common when we're on the road, and each one eats away at our limited attention.

Dr. Miller says we mistakenly believe we're paying attention to everything around us when we multi-task.

A 1999 study by psychologists Simons and Chabris illustrates Miller's point. Participants watched a video of six people passing basketballs, and counted how many times the players wearing white passed the ball. Halfway through the video, a woman in a gorilla suit walked onto the screen. In full view, she stood in the middle of the players and beat her chest, and then left. Amazingly, about 50% of the participants did not even notice the gorilla.[xv]

Simons and Chabris called this phenomenon "inattentional blindness", the failure to notice something we aren't expecting – even when we're looking directly at it.

Half the participants of the "invisible gorilla" study were demonstrating inattentional blindness the way drivers do when their attention is spread across primary and distracting tasks.

In a follow-up experiment, the researchers asked participants to track passes made through the air and passes that were bounced. Twenty percent more of this group failed to notice the gorilla. An increase in the task load made it harder to notice unexpected objects. Perception was all the more impaired.[xvi]

In 1995, Boston police officer Kenneth M. Conley was chasing a shooting suspect who climbed over a fence. During the pursuit, he passed a violent assault between two people. Officer Conley did not stop to intervene. He claimed he didn't see the incident. He was put on trial for alleged negligence. Years later he was vindicated on the basis of inattentional blindness.

Simons and Chabris conducted another interesting experiment, this time with students who were told to go on a three-minute run, keep a steady distance behind the person in front of them, and count the number of times the runners in front of them touched their heads to wipe off sweat. Once again, results showed that people can falsely believe they are good multi-taskers. The evidence? A fight was staged along the running path, and approximately 35% of the students did not notice it.[xvii]

The results do not indicate that one person can multi-task and another cannot. Rather, they indicate that we are not always alert to what seems obvious to others, and this probably has to do with the particular way we happen to be spreading our attention across tasks at a particular time and how we are thinking about them. In other words, any of us might see the "invisible gorilla" in one situation but miss the staged fight in another. If we decide to concentrate on noticing the tricky events, our attention will be pulled away from other things because we are always working with a finite amount of attention.

We should think about the factors of inattentional blindness, because they relate to distracted driving. Let's consider a few of them.

Obviousness. This has to do with the object's ability to catch our attention. For example: especially on a rainy day, a gray car pulling out in front of your car would not be as conspicuous as a bright red car.

Expectation. When we expect certain things to happen, we might overlook or block out what actually *is* happening. For example, if we expect the car up the road to be moving, when it's really stalled, we may not realize we're approaching the stalled vehicle at high speed.

Capacity. As stated earlier, we can spread our attention around only so far. Even when we are expert at something, the activity consumes a certain amount of attention. Newer drivers devote greater attention to many tasks that experienced drivers do with little conscious effort. In fact, teens are responsible for a large portion of distracted driving deaths and injuries. Talking on the phone, texting, dialing – each demands part of our mental capacity and can easily compete for the same resources we need for staying aware of our surroundings.

After an accident, people usually assume it wasn't their fault. As injury attorneys, we've often heard in depositions, "I was looking left, right, left, and then the other guy came out of nowhere and all of a sudden he was right on me." It is common for people to say, "I never saw him."

We all know that this simply cannot be true. Cars do not appear out of thin air traveling at full speed. While we cannot be sure how many of these situations may have been a result of inattentional blindness, it seems reasonable to believe that people really did look and yet they did not see the other vehicle.

Distractions Can Cause Blindness

Distractions can blind the mind to things happening around us. When we consider our natural limitations and the serious responsibility of driving safely for everyone's sake – not to mention our own – it's hard to argue that it's okay to use a cellphone while driving. One thing's for sure – the victim of an accident involving a driver who was texting or talking on the phone at the time will not listen to a justification. Neither will a court, an attorney, or an insurance company.

Using technology such as headphones or phones built into the dashboard might possibly reduce the physical nature of cellphone distraction, but "less dangerous" implies that danger is still present.

I, Steven, have been realizing lately that when I used my car's built-in phone system it required me to take my eyes off the road for a brief moment to select the contact I was going to call.

You May Never Notice Your Blindness

You may not realize that you are blind to objects around you at certain times. People generally consider themselves excellent at driving while talking on the phone. Not everyone swerves from lane to lane while talking on the phone. Most people certainly will not admit to swerving when they do, and sometimes it's because they don't even notice they're swerving!

People continue to operate their vehicles while having phone conversations because they assume that, if the two tasks were unsafe together, the drivers would find some sort of supporting evidence in their own daily lives.

An analysis of many studies has found that talking on the phone while driving does not affect people's ability to stay in their lane, maintain appropriate speeds, or keep a good distance between them and the car in front of them.[xviii] However, people's response time in demanding situations is significantly increased.

In other words, you may feel like you are driving perfectly safe, and in many ways you are. You may be able to have a conversation on the phone and get to your destinations safely your entire life.

In an email, psychologist Daniel Simons wrote:

"People tend to be overconfident in their abilities, and the most overconfident also tend to be the least competent (the so-called Dunning-Kruger effect). For cell phones, staying on the road isn't the only issue, and it's not necessarily the familiar stuff that is most problematic. Rather, the biggest risk comes from the unexpected things, the ones we're slower to notice (or don't notice at all) when distracted. In fact, familiarity might actually induce complacency. There are far too many accidents in which people back out of their garage and hit a child in their driveway. Not much could be more familiar and routine than backing out of a driveway, but that doesn't mean we notice everything."[xix]

By having those phone calls, you are putting yourself at an increased risk of inattentional blindness and increasing your response time to critical events. You may not see a car pull out in front of you, but even if you do your reaction time is going to be affected by your choice to talk on the phone.

Is it worth placing yourself, and more importantly, others at greater risk for that phone call?

Let's consider this another way.

Imagine driving down the road with your kids or grandkids (if you don't have any, imagine someone special in the car with you). You are on your way to a party, a joyful celebration. Do you want the drivers in other cars to intentionally place you and your loved ones at greater risk because they wanted to have a phone conversation? If you were in an accident and someone was injured or killed because someone was on the phone and didn't see you or was incapable of reacting fast enough to stop safely – *then* might you have a different opinion about cellphone use?

The science behind the effects of cellphone conversations is based on the psychology of how the mind works, not people's own opinions and their confidence in how they think their mind operates.

The negative effects of cellphone conversations on the road are real – even if you have had no personal experience with them. Perhaps you have been fortunate enough not to have been placed in a situation that tested your mind beyond its limits.

We all engage in activities that place ourselves at increased risk, and that is up to the individual to decide. But our decisions can place others at increased risk without their consent.

Note: For readers interested in learning more about misconceptions that nearly all of us have about how our minds operate, we recommend the book, The Invisible Gorilla *by Daniel Simons and Christopher Chabris. It is an easy, fun read that explores how our mind works. Many fascinating experiments back up their claims.*

Legal Ramifications

States are enacting legislation to ban various kinds of cellphone use. A handful of states have no bans at all on it. Indiana has a ban on texting for all drivers and a ban on all cellphone use for novice drivers. New York has a similar ban on texting and has banned handheld cellphone use for all drivers.

(We recommend that you investigate your state's laws to make sure you are in compliance. Repercussions can be severe.)

In familiar terms, the principal danger of cellphone use is based in sensory overload. We ask you, therefore, does it make sense to stress your mental capacity with the distraction of a phone conversation, texting, or other cellphone activities? And does it make sense to have laws banning handheld use?

Let's investigate.

Do bans on hand-held cellphone use affect drivers' behavior? Yes. Studies following up on New York, Connecticut, and the District of Columbia's bans years ago estimate that the amount of hand-held use was reduced between approximately 25% and 75%.[xx] In 2009 the Insurance Institute for Highway Safety (IIHS) conducted a phone survey and found that in states with bans on hand-held use, 56% of respondents reported cellphone use while driving. In states without bans, 69% reported using their phones while driving.[xxi]

It appears that bans on hand-held use do affect driving behavior, but do these bans result in fewer crashes?

Ross Rader, senior vice-president of the IIHS, points out, "It's not surprising that lawmakers are focused on phone use, because it's such a visible manifestation of distracted driving. The bottom line is that there's no evidence so far that various kinds of cell phone restrictions around the country have actually reduced crashes."[xxii]

It is difficult to know which crashes were the result of someone talking on the phone unless the evidence is discovered in a lawsuit. People involved in an accident do not typically hop out of their vehicle and confess that they had been talking on their cellphone when the crash happened. To assess whether or not bans have an influence on accidents we can look at insurance claims. If insurance claims decrease after a ban, then it would be prudent to look deeper to see if there is a connection. If insurance claims stay the same or increase, it is safe to assume that the bans are not solving the problem.

(It is possible that bans could be causing a new problem, where drivers are trying extra hard not to be noticed when texting or talking on the phone.)

One study assessed four states' data from before and after they enacted hand-held bans. One state had no significant change while three had significant increases.[xxiii] Another study reviewed data from three states and the District of Columbia and found two without significant changes and two increases.[xxiv]

If the issue were simply about people holding a phone to talk, then we could expect to find statistical data showing that the decrease in people's handheld use following bans would result in a decrease in accidents, measured by a decrease in insurance claims. However, there is no statistical data showing that these bans are affecting our citizens' safety.

Let's revisit our question: Does it make sense to have laws banning handheld use? Billboards, campaigns, and legislation have been introduced to curb the deaths suffered at the hands of drivers willfully engaging in the distracting activity of talking on the phone. But no statistical analysis has shown that we are making significant progress on this front.

A Judge Weighs In

Let's consider another way our judicial system is influencing this topic.

A New Jersey appeals court recently ruled that a person who sends a text to a driver can share liability if a driver receiving the text message causes an accident.

A panel of judges on the Superior Court of New Jersey's Appellate division found that the sender would be liable if the person had a "special reason" to know the recipient was driving and would read the messages.

The ruling was in the case of a couple who lost their legs when their motorcycle was hit by a teenager who was texting and driving in Morris County, NJ in 2009. The motorists had sued the teen driver's girlfriend who sent him the text messages.

The appeals court said a person who texts a motorist cannot normally be held liable for the driver's negligent actions. The court said, however, that the texter has a duty to refrain from texting if he or she knows that the recipient is driving a car and is likely to read the message.

The court wrote:

"The sender of a text message has a duty under the common law of negligence to refrain from sending a text to a person who the sender knows, or has special reason to know, is then driving and is likely to read the text while driving.[xxv]

"The texter has a duty to users of the public roads to refrain from sending the driver a text at that time."[xxvi]

The injured couple settled their lawsuit against the driver for $500,000, but were unsuccessful in the claim against the texting girlfriend. Notice, however, that the court's opinion indicated that the claim would indeed have been successful if the victims had been able to present the required proof. Simply put, the texter can share responsibility for damages.

Considering Liability

As injury attorneys, we are not sure it is likely that someone sending a text message with knowledge that the other person is driving and is likely to read or respond to it would result in liability. A lawsuit takes on more complexity when an additional person is included like that. For example, you must determine what percentage of the accident's damages should be held against the one who sent the text.

If I know that you're driving and I send you a text that I believe you will look at or respond to, and it is foreseeable that I will cause you to be distracted, my action may be considered negligent. That is arguably a breach of reasonability. However, the next question is, Did my act contribute to this accident?

The fact that you looked at the text was an intervening cause that ultimately led to the accident. But you did not *have* to look at it.

Trying to hold the texter liable for the accident is a slippery slope. It's similar to dram shop liability, in which bars can be found responsible for selling alcohol to patrons who displayed signs of being intoxicated and afterwards get in an accident.

Regardless of whether you agree with the New Jersey court's ruling, it is important to know and understand it, because more judges are likely to consider that court's ruling when deciding cases.

Take the Pledge

Sean was the kid nearly every teacher found difficult. You might think his problematic behavior throughout grade school was a reflection of his intelligence, but it wasn't. All through middle school he managed to have so many detentions and "Saturday schools" that he was at school more than most of the teachers and the other students. In high school, he aced nearly every biology test while maintaining a failing grade, because he refused to do homework and other assignments outside of class.

Sean wasn't a pain for every teacher. His grade-school Spanish teacher had very little trouble with him or any other problem students. What was the difference? In Señor Russell's classroom there was a cooperative culture of energetic learning. Acting out disrupted the learning activities, and most students preferred to preserve the enjoyable learning environment. While many other teachers were busy trying to lay down the law, Señor Russell established a culture in which students volunteered appropriate behavior.

That's what we need to do on our roads – establish a culture in which people want to drive as smart as possible for everyone's sake. We need passengers and callers to be equally concerned, because drivers and laws themselves may never solve the problem of distracted driving.

Statistics affect people's view of things. When I, Luke, first started working on this topic, I found that approximately 3,300 people die each year from distracted driving in the United States.[xxvii] Compared to our national population of more than 300,000,000, a number like 3,300 seems rather small. You might think you'd never cause one of those fatalities or be one of them. But somebody's causing them and somebody's getting killed. Still, it's hard to believe we will be one of those numbers.

In Jonah Berger's recent, best-selling book *Contagious*, he tells about a campaign to affect student drinking at the University of Arizona. The campaign first attempted to shift the student body's attitude by using posters and ads focusing on the dangers of binge drinking. They even showed how alcohol affects performance in school. These statistics had little to no effect on the student body's attitude. [xxviii]

Eventually the school took a new route and conducted a survey that discovered that most students did not approve of the excess known as binge drinking by their peers. While the majority of the student body appeared to be on board with a culture of binging, the reality was that most in fact were not and most were not binging.

When the campaign turned the focus on this new information, the students' behavior began changing. They were affected by the revelation that their peers were not drinking as much as they thought and that their peers did not approve of the drinking behavior. Students accepted a new culture that was much more in line with their inner thinking.

Culture is made of thinking and doing. When it comes to distracted driving, we need a change in our thinking in order to have safer behavior on the road. A sweeping change won't happen overnight; there will be many more victims. But we can start this very moment to make our roads safer.

An abundance of research shows that distracted driving is a serious issue. Adults generally agree that cellular use while driving is dangerous. However, a study by Nationwide Insurance revealed that 98% of Americans claim to be "safe drivers" while 80% of drivers have been guilty of, and witnesses to, driving while distracted.[xxix]

Similarly, a large portion of Americans are mixing cellphones with driving, yet more than 80% of drivers say that drivers using cell phones are a serious or extremely serious traffic safety problem. More than 50% say the problem is unacceptable.[xxx]

When talking to people about distracted driving, we found that they often refer to "that other person" who is holding up traffic while talking on the phone. They don't see themselves as the problem. A close friend confessed that he doesn't want his wife to talk on the phone while driving, but when he receives a call on the road he answers it.

As a group, our culture agrees that distracted driving is serious and dangerous. As individuals we prefer to say the other person is the real problem. We enjoy a false sense of security about being able to drive with sensory overload, while that irresponsible driver in the other car should be pulled over and maybe even arrested for doing so.

Gacovino Lake invites everyone to go to www.DriveCellFree.net and take the pledge to drive cell-free. We can all influence people around us by simply sharing our choice to drive cell-free. You don't need to preach. Just share what you've been learning and thinking in regard to cognitive limitations and multi-tasking, and how it's unfair to gamble with other people's safety.

We may be up against a giant – that is to say, up against the popular perception that people are excellent "multi-taskers" and that we are mentally capable of driving and using our phones without endangering others. But we can beat this giant.

It starts with you.

And it continues with you.

Join us at www.DriveCellFree.net. Most of all, we invite you to be a positive influence by sharing your safe driving lifestyle with those around you. We can save a lot of heartache and loss.

If you would like to order physical copies of this book, you can purchase them on Amazon for the lowest price possible. We do not make any money from our books on Amazon. We've priced them as low as possible so that people will share them with friends, family, and colleagues.

If you are interested in bulk quantities of this book for your organization, please contact Luke W Russell at: L.Russell@gacovinolake.com.

The digital version of this book is available for free on our website www.DriveCellFree.net and on Amazon Kindle.

Help for Victims

Accidents are an unpleasant and unfortunate part of life. Losing someone you love is painful, to say the least, especially when you feel that another person is responsible. The Law Offices of Gacovino Lake have served more than 20,000 clients across the nation over the last twenty years, and we are here as a resource for victims of distracted driving. If you or a loved one has been in an accident and you feel that the other driver may be at fault, our team is available to you.

Call to speak with someone immediately: (800) 550-0000.

Or request a free case review at:
www.NationwideInjuryAttorneys.com

About the Authors

Attorneys Steven D. Gacovino and Edward Lake started their law firm, Gacovino Lake, in 1993. For 20 years they have served over 20,000 individuals across the nation recovering hundreds of millions in compensation for their clients. They represent victims in cases of distracted driving, auto accidents, and other injuries. They also help victims of defective medical devices (e.g., metal hip implants) and medications (e.g., Tylenol®).

Luke W Russell began producing marketing materials for Gacovino Lake in early 2012. A home-grown Hoosier, Luke brings a desire to investigate legal topics that are not well understood by the public. Some of these topics appear in his "You Be the Judge" video series.

Bibliography

[i] United States. NHTSA. *What is Distracted Driving?* Washington, D.C., Web. <http://www.distraction.gov/content/get-the-facts/facts-and-statistics.html>.
[ii] United States. NHTSA. *What is Distracted Driving?* Washington, D.C., Web. <http://www.distraction.gov/content/get-the-facts/facts-and-statistics.html>.
[iii] "AT&T Teen Driver Survey." *AT&T.* N.p., n.d. Web. 17 Dec 2013. <http://www.att.com/Common/about_us/txting_driving/att_teen_survey_exe cutive.pdf>.
[iv] United States. National Safety Council. *National Safety Council Estimates that At Least 1.6 Million Crashes Each Year Involve Drivers Using Cell Phones and Texting* . 2012. Web. <http://www.nsc.org/Pages/NSCestimates16millioncrashescausedbydriversusi ngcellphonesandtexting.asp&xgt;.
[v] "New data from Virginia Tech Transportation Institute provides insight into cell phone use and driving distraction." *Virginia Tech.* N.p., 29 Jul 2009. Web. 17 Dec 2013. <http://www.vtnews.vt.edu/articles/2009/07/2009-571.html>.
[vi] United States. National Safety Council. *Estimating the Costs of Unintentional Injuries, 2011.* Itasca, IL, 2011. Web. <http://www.nsc.org/nsc_library/Documents/Estimating the Cost of Unintentional Injuries, 2011.pdf>.
[vii] Tison, J.; Chaudhary, N.; and Cosgrove, L. 2011. National phone survey on distracted driving attitudes and behaviors. Report no. DOT HS 811-555. Washington, DC: U.S. Department of Transportation.

viii "Distracted driving study: Cell phone dialing, texting dangerous. Talking? Less so.." CBS News. N.p., 02 Jan 2014. Web. 13 Jan 2014. <http://www.cbsnews.com/news/distracted-driving-study-cell-phone-dialing-texting-dangerous-talking-less-so/>.

ix "DRIVER DISTRACTION IN COMMERCIAL VEHICLE OPERATIONS." US Department of Transportation. N.p., n.d. Web. 13 Jan 2014. <http://www.distraction.gov/research/PDF-Files/Driver-Distraction-Commercial-Vehicle-Operations.pdf>.

x Horowitz, Todd, auth. "The Risks of Hands-Free Phones." *Science Update*. N.p., 02 Jan 2009. web. 17 Dec 2013. <http://audio.scienceupdate.com/podcast/090102_sciup_pod.mp3>.

xi Scholl, Brian, Nicholaus Noles, Vanya Pasheva, and Rachel Sussman. *"Talking on a cellular telephone dramatically increases 'sustained inattentional blindness'."* Journal of Vision. N.p., 22 Oct 2003. Web. 18 Dec 2013. <http://www.journalofvision.org/content/3/9/156>.

xii Chabris, Christopher, and Daniel Simons. *The Invisible Gorilla: How Our Intuitions Deceive Us*. 1. New York: Random House LLC, 2009. 7. Print.

xiii Chabris, Christopher, and Daniel Simons. *The Invisible Gorilla: How Our Intuitions Deceive Us*. 1. New York: Random House LLC, 2009. 15. Print.

xiv Hamilton, Jon. "Think You're Multitasking? Think Again."*NPR*. N.p., 02 Oct 2008. Web. 17 Dec 2013. <http://www.npr.org/templates/story/story.php?storyId=95256794>.

xv Chabris, Christopher, and Daniel Simons. "The Invisible Gorilla." *The Invisible Gorilla*. N.p. Web. 17 Dec 2013. <http://www.theinvisiblegorilla.com/gorilla_experiment.html>.

xvi Chabris, Christopher, and Daniel Simons. *The Invisible Gorilla: How Our Intuitions Deceive Us*. 1. New York: Random House LLC, 2009. 24. Print.

xvii Chabris, Christopher, Adam Weinberger, Matthew Fontaine, and Daniel J. Simons. "You do not talk about Fight Club if you do not notice Fight Club: Inattentional blindness for a simulated real-world assault." *i-Perception*. N.p., 17 Apr 2011. Web. 17 Dec 2013. <http://i-perception.perceptionweb.com/fulltext/i02/i0436.pdf>.

xviii Horrey, W.J. and Wickens, C.D. 2006. Examining the impact of cell phone conversations on driving using meta-analytic techniques. Human Factors 48(1):196-205.

xix Simons, Daniel. "Are you interested in a phone interview?" Message to Luke W Russell. 28 Jan 2014. E-mail.

xx McCartt, A.T.; Hellinga, L.A.; Strouse, L.M.; and Farmer, C.M. 2010. Long-term effects of handheld cell phone laws on driver handheld cell phone use. Traffic Injury Prevention 11(2):133-41.

xxi Braitman, K.A. and McCartt, A.T. 2010. National reported patterns of driver cellphone use. Traffic Injury Prevention 11(6):543-8.

xxii Stirling, Stephen. "Distracted driving still a problem, despite attempts to curtail cell phone use behind the wheel." N.J.com. N.p., 27 Jun 2012. Web. 13 Jan 2014. <http://www.nj.com/news/index.ssf/2012/06/distracted_driving_still_a_pro.html>.

xxiii Highway Loss Data Institute. 2010. Texting laws and collision claim frequencies. HLDI Bulletin 27(11). Arlington, VA.

xxiv Trempel, R. E.; Kyrychenko, S. Y.; and Moore, M. J. 2011. Does banning hand-held cell phone use while driving reduce collisions? Chance 24(3):6-11.

xxv New Jersey. New Jersey Courts. 2013. Web. <http://www.judiciary.state.nj.us/opinions/squibs12-13.pdf>.

xxvi Gershman, Jacob. "Senders of Texts to Drivers Can Be Held Liable, Court Rules." *The Wall Street Journal*. N.p., 27 Aug 2013. Web. 17 Dec 2013. <http://blogs.wsj.com/law/2013/08/27/senders-of-texts-to-drivers-can-be-held-liable-court-rules/>.

xxvii United States. National Highway Traffic Safety Administration. *Distracted Driving 2011*. 2013. Web. <http://www-nrd.nhtsa.dot.gov/Pubs/811737.pdf>.

xxviii Berger, Jonah. *Contagious: Why Things Catch On*. New York: Simon & Schuster, 2013. 132-133. Print.

xxix "Almost All Americans Believe They Are Safe Drivers." Nationwide Insurance, 18 May 2008. Web. 17 Dec 2013. <http://www.prweb.com/releases/driving/percent/prweb954104.htm>.

xxx "Cell Phones and Driving: Research Update." *AAA Foundation for Traffic Safety*. N.p., n.d. Web. 17 Dec 2013. <https://www.aaafoundation.org/sites/default/files/CellPhonesandDrivingReport.pdf>.

10992390R00024